Level 4-5
(Intermediate/Upper Intermediate)

Best of Strauss

For Piano Solo

Arranged by John W. Schaum and Wesley Schaum

Foreword

Johann Strauss, Jr. famous as the "Waltz King," came from a musical family of composers and dance band conductors. He is sometimes known as Johann Strauss II or Johann Strauss the Younger. His father, brother and son were all musicians. The Strauss family was connected with Austrian court music for nearly a century.

Although best known for his waltzes (he wrote over 400), Strauss also composed operettas and numerous polkas, marches, quadrilles and other pieces. To show his versatility, this book includes several marches, polkas, and music from his best known operettas, "Die Fledermaus" ("The Bat") and "Gypsy Baron."

All music in this collection was originally composed for orchestra and has been transcribed for the piano. The waltzes were written as lengthly medleys of five or six different themes. These arrangements use only one or two of the most familiar themes from each waltz.

Index

Acceleration Waltz, Op. 234	22
Annen Polka, Op. 117 (sometimes called "French Polka")	16
Artist's Life, Op. 316	10
Blue Danube, Op. 314	2
March (from "Gypsy Baron", Op. 417)	12
Persian March, Op. 289	20
Tales from the Vienna Woods, Op. 325	14
Thousand and One Nights, Op. 346	18
Tritsch-Tratsch Polka, Op. 214	8
Vienna Life, Op. 354	5
You and You (from "Die Fledermaus," Op 367)	6

Schaum Publications, Inc. • 10235 N. Port Washington Rd. • Mequon, WI 53092 • www.schaumpiano.net

© Copyright 1969 and 2010 by Schaum Publications, Inc., Mequon, Wisconsin
International Copyright Secured • All Rights Reserved • Printed in U.S.A.
ISBN-13: 978-1-936098-18-7

Warning: The reproduction of any part of this publication without prior written consent of Schaum Publications, Inc. is prohibited by U.S. Copyright Law and subject to penalty. This prohibition includes all forms of printed media (including any method of photocopy), all forms of electronic media (including computer images), all forms of film media (including filmstrips, transparencies, slides and movies), all forms of sound recordings (including cassette tapes and compact disks), and all forms of video media (including video tapes and DVD).

Blue Danube

Vienna Life

You and You

from "Die Fledermaus"

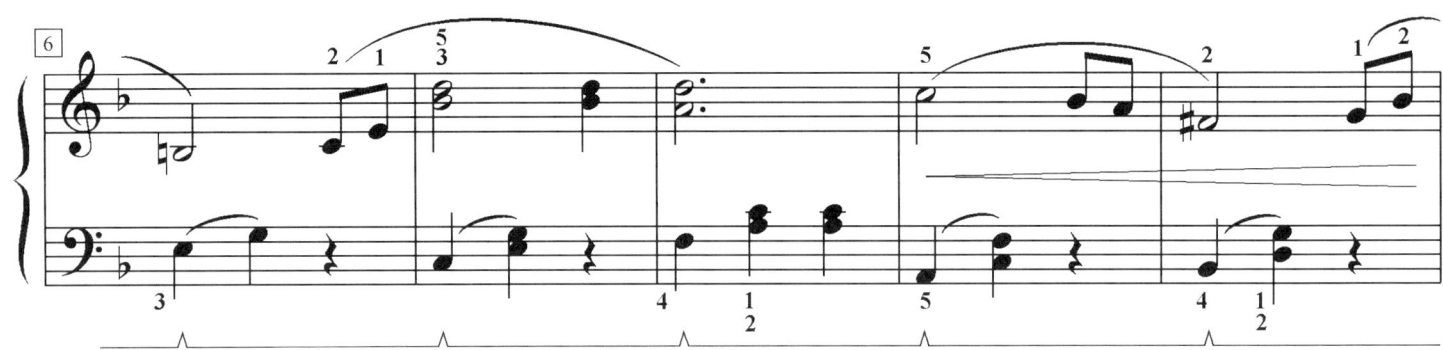

Tritsch-Tratsch Polka

Artist's Life

March

from "Gypsy Baron"

Tales from the Vienna Woods

Annen Polka

* The small wedge shaped mark placed over or under a note head is the symbol for ***martellato*** (mahr-tel-LAH-toh). It means to play with a heavy hammer-like staccato touch.

Thousand and One Nights

Persian March

Acceleration Waltz